Spring Scenes

COLORING BOOK

Teresa Goodridge

DOVER PUBLICATIONS
GARDEN CITY, NEW YORK

The world comes alive when April showers bring May flowers. You'll practically smell the fresh green grass and feel that first warm breeze of the year as you flip through the 31 illustrations in this coloring book. Try using different media and techniques as you color picnic baskets, fields of flowers, peaceful meadows, and lush plant life. Birds, bunnies, dogs, and horses all help you welcome in the season! Pages are perforated and unbacked to make removing and displaying your work easy.

Bibliographical Note

Spring Scenes Coloring Book is a new work,
first published by Dover Publications in 2016.

International Standard Book Number
ISBN-13: 978-0-486-81412-4
ISBN-10: 0-486-81412-2

Manufactured in the United States of America
81412215   2023
www.doverpublications.com